Veli Ndaba

YOU'RE BORN TO WIN

So go ahead and reach your true potential!

Copyright ©Veli Ndaba 2014

All rights reserved. No part of this publication may be reproduced, stored in a retrieval system, or transmitted in any form or by any means, electronic, mechanical, photocopying, recording or otherwise, without the prior permission of the publishers.

Cover design by Dylan Fourie (Boksburg)

Editing & proofreading by Eulália Snyman (Alberton)
Graphics & page layout by Marco van der Walt (Alberton) Printed by Business Print, www.businessprint.co.za (Pretoria) Photographs by Photo Maria Studio (Pretoria)

A South African publication

# Contents

Endorsements ................................................................ 4

About Veli Ndaba ........................................................... 6

Searching For Destiny ..................................................... 9

Stepping Toward Success............................................. 12

All You've Been Waiting For ........................................ 17

The Fear Factor ............................................................ 22

Dealing With Change ................................................... 27

Importance of Setting Goals ........................................ 32

Now Is The Time........................................................... 41

Healthy Is Indeed Wealthy ........................................... 49

Reinventing Yourself.................................................... 56

Step-By-Step................................................................. 56

Secret Success Formula................................................ 62

Taking Responsibility for You ...................................... 73

A note on winning........................................................ 79

Acknowledgements ..................................................... 81

References and suggested reading.............................. 82

# Endorsements

"The book is well written and easy to read! I could not put it down. It speaks to people at different levels and with different IQs, proving that IQ has little to do with success. Only one's choice is key." ~ Mahlatse Letsoala, former group HR director at Bayer Group South Africa.

"Truly inspiring!" ~ Carina van der Walt, editor of the Alberton Record newspaper, Alberton.

"Veli is a passionate soul whose very presence demands that you be inspired: Talking with Veli makes you want to go out there and change your life, as well as remove all those thoughts of selfdoubt and make those things happen that you've been putting off all your life. What an inspirational person, and what an inspirational book. Go on, buy this book: It took me one hour to read, but will make a difference for the rest of my life." ~ Philip Kassel, Certified Financial Planner®, Bruma, Johannesburg.

"You'll leave this body of work inspired to pursue your best self." ~ Timothy Webster, international speaker, personal brand specialist and author.

"South Africa is currently in a period where it is facing numerous challenges, however, the change to improve is something that has to come from South Africans themselves. What a perfect opportunity to have Veli's book as a tool to assist South Africans to become a winning nation," ~ Lerato K Masha, Gauteng regional operations manager at Nampak Tubes & Megapak.

# About Veli Ndaba

Veli Ndaba was born in Soweto. He studied at the University of South Africa [Bachelor of Science in Management Science] and at the University of Johannesburg [National Diploma in Mechanical Engineering] and embarked on a career in the corporate world.

Through hard work and dedication, he soon reached managerial level. However, he felt something was amiss. "I did not feel alive. It was as if something was suffocating me, and I knew I had to make a change. After all, if we do not move forward, life will just move on without us," he says.

In 2011 he started his own business, specialising in corporate training, life and business coaching. He joined communication and leadership organisation Toastmasters, eventually became president of his local club and now gives motivational talks around the country.

Veli Ndaba lives in Alberton, a town situated about 20 kms from Johannesburg. He is a family man; he is married to Mpumi and has two sons, Ntokozo and Sanele.

Contact Veli via email veli@velindaba.co.za or via LinkedIn.

# Success

If you want a thing bad enough to go out and fight for it, to work day and night for it, to give up your time, your peace and sleep for it …

If all that you dream and scheme is about it… and life seems useless and worthless without it …

If you gladly sweat for it and fret for it and plan for it and lose all your terror of the opposition for it …

If you simply go after that thing that you want with all your capacity, strength and sagacity, faith, hope and confidence and stern pertinacity

If neither cold, poverty, famine, nor gout, sickness nor pain, of body and brain, can keep you away from the thing that you want … if dogged and grim you beseech and beset it, with the help of God, YOU WILL GET IT!

…. Poem by Berton Braley, (American poet 1882 – 1966)

# Searching For Destiny

*"Don't be discouraged; it is often the last key in the bunch that opens the lock." - Unknown*

When you see someone searching, scratching, moving stuff, checking underneath furniture and relentlessly probing everywhere, you start wondering. Like any 'normal' person, you're likely to ask, WHAT ARE YOU SEARCHING FOR? Or you will ask someone who is nearby, WHAT IS HE SEARCHING FOR?

The act of searching is hard to hide - it usually attracts attention, even from strangers. And interestingly, most of us are willing to help those who are searching for something.

So, what are you looking for? If you've picked up this book, it means that you are a searching soul. I bet that you - like most people - are searching for a long list of things, starting with money, health, love and happiness as the most important.

You may be looking for purpose, for your destiny. Most

of all, you are probably looking to be the best you. To reach your full potential, your greatness. To feel like a winner. I believe that all this, and more, is within your reach: search and you will find!

During my different encounters and interventions, people often tell me that what stops them from achieving their greatness, is the fact that other people won't help them. "You know how it goes," they say with a shake of the head. "When it comes to the crunch, everybody is too busy to help you! You know how people are."

I know how people are. We are afraid of being great. We are lazy. But at some point we run out of excuses. For me the turning point was the day I declared, I AM TIRED OF LIVING A SMALL LIFE, I DESERVE BETTER.

I started searching for a better life and a better me. I did not know how I was going to get it, but I refused to give up.

Friends, family and acquaintances saw me searching and were inquisitive enough to ask me, WHAT ARE YOU SEARCHING FOR? I told them that I was searching for my dream and my destiny. Guess what? Some helped me and others referred me to those who later helped me.

Today, I am living my dream. Offering motivational talks at organisations, coaching individuals (life and business), conducting training at big corporations as well as inspiring SMEs and making a difference wherever I am and in whatever I do. For me this is what it means to win and I feel like I have won the lotto. It wouldn't have been possible for me if I hadn't searched.

Make no mistake, I am still not in the same money league as Warren Buffet. Nor am I as well-known as Steve Jobs. I still don't have all the answers to the big questions in life. But I have learnt a couple of things that I'd love to share with you in this book. That is my purpose, to help others reach their full potential. Because I believe that each and every one of us was born to win.

Veli Ndaba

# Stepping Toward Success

*"We are all self-made but only the successful will admit it."*

~ Earl Nightingale

I am immensely glad that you are reading this book. It means that you are taking a crucial step towards the success you've always dreamed of. When you finish this book, you will have learned that success is a science and that you can create your very own success.

Human beings have a success instinct. It is a pity that we don't realise it, isn't it? If you are reading this book, chances are, you want to improve your quality of life. You are tired of looking at acquaintances and strangers and wondering what they are doing differently or better than you. You are tired of living a small life and you believe you can do better.

There's nothing worse than seeing someone who is not as smart as you are, living a better quality life than you are. Why are some people more successful than you?

Know this: it's not their IQ, childhood or networking ability that sets successful people apart, but it's the scientific principles they apply because they learnt that success is a science. World authority on leadership psychology Tony Robbins said, "Success leaves clues". In this book we take a closer look at these clues and at the science of success.

Success means different things to different people, but in a nutshell its true meaning is achieving your goals. So the first and most important step is to define exactly what goals you want to achieve. Success begins with your decision of what it is that you really want and then dedicating yourself wholeheartedly to attaining it.

It sounds a little vague and abstract, so let's add some more flesh to the concept. Success has the following seven basic ingredients:

## 1. Peace of mind

We have the little voice inside of us, the voice of reason that silently guides us to our higher calling. When our lives are in alignment with this voice, we experience self-fulfilment and peace of mind. Misalignment on the other hand leads to frustration, dissatisfaction, stress and illnesses resulting in early death.

## 2. Health and energy

You can achieve all kinds of things in the material world, but at the absence of good health, you will not derive any pleasure from your achievements. Make a deliberate effort to take good care of your health because it fuels your energy and your life.

## 3. Happy relationships

You need to have and sustain happy relationships with the people you love and those that care about you. In fact, the ability to maintain long- term relationships leads to success.

## 4. Financial freedom

This means you are making enough money so you don't need to think about it. Many of us worry about money all the time and that is a lousy way to live. We think about money when we wake up, during the day, and when we go to sleep at night and sometimes it even keeps us awake at night! The only way for you to achieve financial freedom is for you to clearly define your financial goals and then devise plans to achieve those goals.

## 5. Worthy goals and ideals

You need to feel that your life stands for something, that you are making a valuable contribution to the world. This world must never be the same again; you must leave a mark, a legacy. You cannot afford to tiptoe through life and go unnoticed.

## 6. Self-awareness

This is how you discover why you react and respond the

way you do to people and situations around you. Successful people understand themselves and why they think and feel the way they do and that's one of the things that you learn, through emotional intelligence. No one is

born with it, but you can learn it. When you understand and accept yourself, you can begin moving forward in other areas of your life.

### 7. Personal fulfilment (self-actualisation)

This is the feeling you get when you become everything that you are capable of becoming; when you realise your full potential for happy living.

Note that nobody chases success for the sake of the chase. Oh no, we all chase success because its benefits are incomparable to other things. Success increases your self-esteem. You like yourself more, you feel more valuable and important. Success helps you achieve a certain level of self-respect that you have never experienced before. You see yourself as an outstanding person. Success also enables you to help others succeed and that makes you even more successful and happy. Remember that:

- Your life gets better when you get better.
- It doesn't matter where you come from; all that matters is where you are going.

- Anything that is worth doing, is worth doing poorly at first until you master it. You can learn anything you need to learn to achieve your goals, for example, business skills, self-development, moneymaking skills, and so on.
- You are only as free as your options or the alternatives that you create for yourself. If it does not work one way, it can work in a different way – try it.
- Within every difficulty you face is a seed of equal or greater benefit or opportunity.
- The only real limits on what you can do, are self-imposed. There are no limits outside, there are only limits on the inside.

When you're successful, you hardly need an alarm clock. You just jump out of bed in the morning because you are optimistic about life and about the future. You know that easy come, easy go. You do things that are deemed hard while other people avoid them. You always seek to get the most out of the day whereas others wonder how they will go through the day.

Some people dream of success while others wake up and start stepping towards it … go ahead and don't stop.

# All You've Been Waiting For

*"There is no man living who isn't capable of doing more than he thinks he can do."* ~ *Henry Ford*

We are all born naked and dumb. As we grow up, we learn to speak, walk, and behave. We don't have much choice in this as we can only learn what we are taught. Have you ever thought about it?

It is a topic that has fascinated humankind forever and a day and has led to movies like Tarzan (where a human child is brought up by animals and copies the behaviour of the animal-parents). There is also the ongoing debate about nature versus nurture - it tackles the question of which is more important: inherited traits or learned behaviour.

The fact of the matter is that you are shaped by both your genetic make- up as well as your upbringing. Your parents, siblings, extended family, community, and teachers have a huge influence in how you see the world and on who you become. The good news, however, is that you have a choice: you can decide who you want to become! You are all you have been waiting for!

In his early years, brilliant scientist Albert Einstein was a poor student who was called mentally slow and unsociable. He went on to win numerous honorary degrees as well as the Nobel Prize for Physics.

Abraham Lincoln's teachers described him as a daydreamer who asked foolish questions. He has gone down in history as the 16th president in the United States and as being instrumental in getting slavery abolished.

Inventor Thomas Edison was called a hopeless case when he was seven years old. His teacher described him as "addled" and said it would be useless for him to continue in school. Edison invented a whole long list of things over and above the light bulb.

There are thousands, if not millions, of such inspiring stories. The common thread is that these great human beings didn't allow others to determine their destiny.

We are born with talents and gifts that make the world a better place. The only problem is that some of us don't fully use these gifts and talents because of the way we were raised and the beliefs that we have developed about ourselves.

Who are you? You are not only what you see in the mirror, but also how you feel inside. Listen to the voice inside of you.

Spiritual guru Dr Howard Thurman who served as spiritual advisor to Dr. Martin Luther King, Jr, spoke of the voice of the genuine:

"There is something in every one of you that waits and listens for the sound of the genuine in yourself. It is the only true guide you will ever have. And if you cannot hear it, you will all of your life spend your days on the ends of strings that somebody else pulls."

Simply put, if you don't listen to the voice in your soul that constantly tells you who you are, you will never be happy and you will live the rest of your life like a prisoner. It is possible to get out of the prison, to overcome obstacles that prevent you from becoming the true you who was born to shine.

Sure, you can't change your height or your blood type. But there is much you can change. You can lose weight and change shape, for example. Most importantly, you can re-programme your mind and change your life. As an adult you have the power of choice, to choose what you want, how you want and when you want it. Look at your life right now – are you happy with yourself? People live their lives according to what they believe about themselves.

Your story may be misleading you. Change the false story about yourself. Ultimately, it does not matter where you were born and how you were raised. What matters is your desire, determination, and your will. You can achieve whatever your heart desires. You are all you've been waiting for.

Don't waste time blaming external factors such as government, politics, weather, parents, teachers, employers, company policy, and so on. And don't waste time doing the same things over and over again.

Albert Einstein said, "Insanity is doing the same thing over and over again and expecting different results."

The mental processes influence the outcome. If you come from a negative environment, you have been programmed to believe you 'cannot'.

Muhammad Ali believed he was the greatest boxer before he became world champion. In the early 1950s, Australian athlete John Landy said repeatedly that it was impossible to run a mile in less than four minutes. He frequently ran it in four minutes 10 seconds, and when he said it was impossible to run it in less time, the world believed him. Guess what happened? In 1954 British athlete Roger Bannister, ran the mile in under four minutes and Landy was suddenly also able to break through the four-minute barrier. The mile was not reduced in length; it was the athletes' belief that changed.

The point is, you achieve what you believe is possible. You must commit to the belief that you were born to shine and achieve whatever your heart desires. William Hutchison Murray said, "Until one is committed, there is hesitancy, the chance to draw back, always ineffectiveness. "

Concerning all acts of initiative (and creation), there is one elementary truth that cannot be ignored: that the moment one definitely commits oneself, then Providence moves too. All sorts of things occur that would never otherwise have occurred. A whole stream of events issues from the decision, raising in your favour all manner of unforeseen incidents and meetings and material assistance, which no man could have

dreamed of. Whatever you can do, or dream you can do, begin it. Boldness has genius, power, and magic in it. Begin it now.

People don't just become good, they become good because they want to be good. It is because of their deliberate commitment to become good that they excel. You have got to be clear in your mind as to how good you want to be. There are different levels of greatness - do you want to be quite good? Good? Very good? Best in your field? Best in the world? Commit and work at it so you can ultimately become whoever you want to be.

After failing 200 times while designing the light bulb, Thomas Edison said, "Of the 200 light bulbs that didn't work, every failure told me something that I was able to incorporate into the next attempt."

Don't let mistakes or failure put you off, soldier on until you are the winner you're born to be.

# The Fear Factor

***"Fear not that your life will come to an end, but that it will never have a beginning."*** *~John Henry Newman.*

Fear is a subtle and destructive emotion. Fear kills dreams, kills hope, and makes you sick. Fear may age you and fear can hold you back from doing something that you know deep in yourself that you are capable of doing. Fear can paralyze you and make you feel as though you're under a hypnotic spell. Fear is nobody's friend.

Yet, most of us listen to the voice of fear. Most of us allow fear to hold us back from what we deserve, from the success that is rightfully ours. What is the benefit of giving up on yourself, of not stepping up, of not taking life head on?

You've got to ask yourself, how long am I going to allow fear to hold me back?

Fear is what holds most people back from achieving their dreams and goals. It is not so much that we fear failure and making mistakes – but rather that we fear that people will think less of us if we make mistakes.

We carry this fear in our heads and it makes us:

- Want to be perfect the first time and every time we do something
- Too timid to try something new
- Avoid and hide mistakes at all costs
- Want everyone to like us
- Want everyone to show support all the time

You must wake up and realise that these things are unrealistic. Come to terms with the fact that you will make mistakes and fail while pursuing your dreams. You will probably also hurt some people's feelings while pursuing your dreams, so, just get over it.

It is said that over 90 percent of the things that we worry about and that hold us back from achieving our dreams, never come to pass. Hence American author and sales guru Zig Ziglar said that FEAR is the acronym for False Evidence Appearing Real. You have to come to terms with the fact that most fears are baseless and useless.

Fear is only useful to you in two instances: 1) when it keeps you safe, for example, it makes you think twice before you overtake another car on the highway; 2) when it forces you into taking action, for example you duck out of the way if you see a cricket ball heading towards you at a high speed.

American entrepreneur and speaker Jim Rohn went from rags to riches and pointed out that, "The few who do, are the envy of the many who watch." Once you conquer fear you will discover that you can do a lot of things. You can achieve a lot of things.

Our beloved Nelson Mandela said, "I learned that courage was not the absence of fear, but the triumph over it. The brave man is not he who does not feel afraid, but he who conquers that fear."

So if you are ready to start living like the winner that you were born to be, think of yourself as a person of courage. You can do it. You are doing it. By reading this book, you have set fear aside and welcomed courage into your life.

Courage not only gives you a good beginning, but also a good future. What's ironic is that both those who don't have courage to take risks and those who have courage to take risks, experience the same amount of fear. The difference is that those who don't take chances, worry about trivial things. If you are going to have to overcome your fear and doubts, you might as well make it count and go big!

Everyone has experienced failure in some way or another. Failure comes in many forms; it occurs whether you act or not. Perhaps by the time you got yourself 'ready' to do something, someone else had taken action – and now you are regretting it.

Regardless of the outcome, I would say that it's far

preferable to fail while doing something than to fail by over-preparing while someone else walks up and scoops up your dreams. This scenario occurs in business every day. People give their fears much more time than they deserve. They wait to make a personal visit or phone call, write an email, or present their proposal because they are afraid of the outcome. Countless individuals share the same excuses for why it is 'not a good time' to take action: It's month-end or beginning of the month. The clients have been in meetings the whole day. They are about to go into meetings. They just bought something. They never return my calls anyway, and so on and so forth …

You just need to take the plunge and do what you fear. In fact, you will be amazed at how much stronger you become and how much more confident you become when you do new things. The person who takes action despite his or her fears, advances the most.

Let's face it, everyone fears something in life. However, it is what we do with that fear that distinguishes us from others. When you allow fear to hold you back, you lose energy, momentum, and confidence – and your fears will almost certainly grow bigger.

It does not take money or luck to create great life; it requires the ability to move past your fears with speed and power. Do not allow fear to settle into any part of your life. It is a defeating attitude and negative emotion.

I look at myself every day and wonder what I would have been and where would I be today had I not taken the decision to follow my heart. I did not wait for better economic conditions, favourable political landscape, better weather conditions, my ducks to be in a row, or to win a lottery.

Instead, I felt the power and listened to the inner voice, which Dr Howard Thurman (considered one of the greatest African American preachers in the early 20th Century) called "the voice of the genuine" which constantly talks to you. I fully realized that no man has the power to stop me when my time has come.

Follow your passion, that thing you would like to do for 24 hours a day and seven days a week without fear or reservation. You were born a winner, remember?

Allow me to quote Jim Rohn once again. This powerful excerpt comes from his book Five Major Pieces To the Life Puzzle:

"It seems that every life form on this planet strives toward its maximum potential ... except human beings. A tree does not grow to half its potential size and then say, 'I guess that will do'. A tree will drive its roots as deep as possible. It will soak up as much nourishment as it can, stretch as high and as wide as nature will allow, and then look down as if to remind us of how much each of us could be come if we would only do all that we can."

# Dealing With Change

**"When one door of happiness closes, another opens; but often we look so long at the closed door that we do not see the one which has been opened for us."**

~ Helen Keller.

As human beings we share the same inevitability: we have to face change. The same was true for everyone who existed in the past and will continue for everyone who will be born in the future. No matter who you are – regardless of your country, race, ethnicity, language, and disposition – change will affect you.

Our lives are in a constant state of transition. Life is always moving forward; nothing ever remains the same. Even those who live essentially quiet lives are affected by change to a greater or lesser extent. We are constantly transported – whether suddenly or gradually

– into the new, the different, the unexpected, or the untried.

We normally experience four types of changes in life, according to the late Dr Myles Munroe of the Bahamas. Dr. Munroe was a pastor, teacher, administrator, author, father, husband and motivational speaker. He travelled throughout the world as a speaker, addressing governments, leaders, businesses, schools/universities and church congregations.

The types of changes are:

- Change that happens around us.
- Change that happens to us.
- Change that happens within us.
- Change that we make happen.

Why is it that only a small percentage of people respond well to change? Most dread change, others refuse to accept it. Some resist it firmly while others regard themselves as victims of change. These approaches are formulas for frustration, depression, and wasted potential.

Dr Munroe used to say that many of us are like the crabs in the Bahamas. The beautiful island country consists of 700 islands in the Atlantic Ocean. The largest island is Andros, and it is famous for its abundance of crabs. Bahamians who live on Andros are known for harvesting crabs and selling them. They normally go crab catching at night because the crabs hide in their holes during the day and come out at night in order to feed.

To catch crabs, Bahamians use a flashlight. This is because when you shine a bright light on the crabs, they freeze as the sudden light shocks them. For a few minutes, they won't move, as if they are paralyzed. The crabs close their eyes, believing that if they can't see you, you can't see them. And so, Bahamians catch crabs by the dozen.

Like these crabs, Most of us prefer to ignore imminent change. Change comes upon us, and startles us. Instead of re-adjusting ourselves to change's bright light, we imagine that if we close our eyes to it, then change can't 'see' us nor affect us. But the reality is that change will 'catch' us and take us with it. Denial is the worst reaction ever – just ask any Bahamian crab!

Change needs to be regarded as a helper, not a destroyer. I went through a lot of changes in my life that pushed me to become the person I am today. I lost my father at the age of 10, my mother when I was 18 and my brother when I was 20. These losses led to great change in my life. They lead to great heartache, but also served to reveal the real person in me that I had not known. I am sure I would not have been this strong and would not have known some of my capabilities if I hadn't gone through these and other life changes.

When they happened to me, I thought I was going to lose my mind. But guess what? I am still alive and much stronger. I have learned to embrace change as my helper and friend. I have learnt to walk by faith and not by sight.

Yes, change can be painful. We cannot deny that. We cry because we lose what we know and we want to cling to what we know. However, for us to reach our full potential and achieve our dreams and goals, we often have to die to who we are and give birth to who we are meant to be.

The four types of changes that we go through in life as described by Dr Myles Munroe, help us get out of our comfort zones, our prison cells. Without change one cannot grow, hence, it is said that life begins at the end of the comfort zone.

Without growth, you cannot be your best and without you being your best, you cannot be happy and reach your full potential. If you don't experience happiness, then you have missed the boat and you haven't really lived fully.

Not only should you welcome change when it comes along, but you should bring about change. You can make 'good' change happen whenever it suits you. What do you do when your old clothes no longer fit? You let go. If something is no longer helping you grow and become what you were born to be, then brother and sister, you must let go and make a change. Have no fear of changing!

You can instantly decide to reprogram and redirect your life toward the level of happiness, success and health that you prefer. These things can happen the moment you invite and embrace change in your life.

You can't successfully reprogram your computer, or your mind, until you change to a new operating system or download some new files … Hit that button to download new software.

Lift your eyes to see the new door of opportunity that has opened for you … it is time for you to change into the winner you were born to be.

# Importance of Setting Goals

*"There are two questions that we have to ask ourselves. The 1st is 'Where am I going?' and the 2nd is 'Who will go with me?' If you ever get these questions in the wrong order, you are in trouble."*

~ Howard Thurman

Most people hope that things will turn out wonderfully one day. Then they get the shock of their lives when things don't turn out that wonderfully at all. Why do things go wrong? Things go awry because people forget to convert their hopes into achievable goals.

It is good to have hope and it is admirable to work hard and be dedicated. However, without setting goals we don't have much of a chance that things will turn out the way we want them to. Without goals, it is impossible for us to have control over the way things turn out and we become exposed to the unpredictability of events, people and even the weather.

Jesus Christ said, "Ask, and it will be given to you; seek, and you will find; knock, and it will be opened to you. For everyone who asks receives, and he who seeks finds, and to him who knocks it will be opened ..." You can read it in the Holy Bible, in the Gospels of Matthew, Luke, James and Mark. It is difficult to grasp and to believe in the fact that you can have almost anything you want. And maybe that is why many of us don't dare go beyond hoping. We don't dare set goals because we don't believe that we are worthy of receiving or achieving great things.

Imagine it is raining outside. And your goal is to scoop enough rain to fill a bath. The amount of rain you catch depends on the size of the container you carry outside, right?

It follows that you will want to carry the biggest container you can possibly find so that you reach your goal of filling a bath. Life is like that. Life allows an abundance of good things – you can call them blessings if you prefer – to rain down on us.

We need to decide which good things we'd like to have and then find a way to get them. Strangely enough, some people carry teaspoons, some carry cups, some buckets, and some drums. The ones carrying teaspoons are usually the ones that complain the most about the fact that life is not fair. They complain about how little they catch, when they should, instead, go fetch a bigger container.

Before you can start setting goals, you have to believe that you are worthy of receiving good things. You need to believe that you are good enough to achieve your goals no matter how ambitious or how humble they may seem to others.

Believe that there is no skill you can't learn; there is no discipline you can't try; there is no class you can't take; and that there's no book you can't read and this belief in your own worth and abilities will propel you forward to do whatever it takes to achieve your goals.

"Make plans like an adult and believe them like a child and incredible things will happen," said Jim Rohn, the hypersuccessful American author, entrepreneur and motivational speaker.

I urge you to please set goals with the heart of a child and not with the mind of a sceptical adult. Every single person has a talent, a skill, or a gift of their own. Some people can draw, some people can dance, some people can make you laugh, and others can move you to tears. People are awesome all round. But I find that most of us fail to look for the awesomeness within ourselves. We tend to focus on what we cannot do, the skills we don't have, and we compare ourselves to others.

You may not be able to do a lot of things that others can do, but so what? That must not stop you from doing the one thing that you can do. That must not stop you from having dreams and from setting goals.

Maybe you can't sing or dance. Maybe you aren't the best cook in the world. Maybe you can't play soccer at competition level. What CAN you do? Focus on what you CAN do and on your personal strengths when you set goals.

The quality of your life, the level of your happiness, the level of your success are determined by the quality of questions you ask yourself. Make the question of "What CAN I do?" be a question you ask and answer frequently and it will change your life as it replaces your limiting beliefs with empowering beliefs.

Take full responsibility for your life. Your goals are yours and you can make them happen. Be wary of, and forgive, friends and family that love and care about you but offer unhelpful advice. They act from a place of fear; they are afraid that you will set 'unrealistic' goals and then suffer disappointment. They will say things like:

- Be careful;
- Play it safe;
- Don't be impractical;
- Success isn't everything;
- Be satisfied with what you have;
- Life is to be lived;
- Money won't make you happy;
- You don't have the necessary experience;
- The economy is bad;
- You don't have enough education;

- You are too young, you are too old.

When you hear people say those things, thank them for their advice and move on. Find comfort in the fact that successful people keep their eyes on their goals regardless of the challenges – and regardless of what others may say.

In his book entitled The University of Success, bestselling author Og Mandino said, "Many of us never realize our greatness because we become side tracked by secondary activity."

We try to do everything and end up spreading ourselves so thin that we make no impact at what we do. Just set a goal and focus on it and give it your all.

# Goal setting exercise

Put a goal setting morning aside for yourself and go sit in a place where you feel at peace and inspired. It can be in a quiet room at home; or it can be at a coffee shop buzzing with activity. Choose whatever works best for you. Preferably do the whole exercise in one sitting. Don't worry if your mind wanders or if you get distracted. Just keep going until you are done.

**What do I want?**

Make a list of things that you aim at. This includes:

- Things that you'd like to own, like a three-bedroom house in Durban
- Things that you'd like to achieve at work, like become the national sales manager for an IT company; or start your own business
- Things that you'd like to achieve in your personal life like have a child or learn to paint. It doesn't matter what it is, as long as it matters to you so much that you dream of it. Be specific and clear. The more you describe your goal, the more it pulls you in the direction you want.

**Why do I want It?**

On your list explain in detail why you want the things that

you want:

- To afford the kind of food I want to eat every day
- To buy R500k house cash
- To be able to send my kid/s to a top private school
- To fulfil a promise I made to my mother
- To donate R100k towards a charity to make the world a better place
- To fulfil a childhood dream

## How am I going to get It?

List all the possible ways that come to mind (without qualifying them):

- Save R1000 every month
- Invest in a popcorn machine and sell popcorn
- Sell bananas
- Invest in the stock market
- Search for a job that will pay you more money.

This list must carry on until about twenty or more ideas, this exercise will also help challenge your brain to become more creative and one of these ideas may change the course of your life.

## When do I want It?

Specify the time frame within which your goal must be achieved, for example 30 October 2016. Time frames force you to be realistic and put your 'how' options (listed above) into perspective. For you to achieve R1-million in two years may be far-fetched if you intend to sell bananas for a living; you'd have to look at other more profitable options.

The elimination process will help you to focus on the realistic options and to identify which are your short-term goals and which are your long-terms goals.

## Who can help me get it?

The fact of life is that no man is an island. Some things you cannot achieve or do on your own. You need to find help from different sources including:

- Family and friends
- Reading relevant books
- Attending conferences and workshops
- Completing a new course
- Consulting a coach and/or mentor - successful people have coaches and mentors, but the unsuccessful ones don't see the need of getting help and this is the main reason why they are not successful!
- Getting rid of people who are negative, toxic

and energy draining and replacing them with people who motivate you and share common goals.

**Wrap it up, write it up!**

When you have completed the above goal setting exercise, summarise it all nicely on paper, on your phone, on your computer and use it as your goal-setting blueprint. Look at your blueprint to remind yourself of your goals. You can also change items or tick them off as you achieve them. Congratulations you have just achieved a MAJOR goal: you have successfully set goals for yourself!

# Now Is The Time

*"Do what you can, with what you have, where you are."* ~ Theodore Roosevelt

I once heard a story about a couple, John and Grace. They were sweethearts at high school and eventually got married when they were in their twenties. They were happy. John worked as a plumber while Grace worked at a supermarket. It looked like everything was going for them.

They had kids and when they reached the ages of 35 and the kids were about 8 and 10 years old, Grace's granny Maggie told her a secret: she said that when she died she would leave everything to them.

John and Grace were ecstatic about their good luck. They started waiting for Gogo 1 Maggie to die. They didn't worry about working harder or saving more because they knew that Gogo Maggie was going to die someday.

Eventually the Gogo died. After the funeral, the family

lawyer started reading her will and revealed that she was so indebted that all she had owned was no longer hers but was 'attached'.

There was nothing to inherit. John and Grace were deeply shocked. They had spent their lives in vain waiting for Gogo Maggie to die!

John and Grace's sad story proves that we cannot sit and wait for things to turn out better one day in the future. It is your life and you have to do the best you can, with what you have, wherever you are right now.

You may be saying: "One day when I win the lottery, I'll start to enjoy life…"

"One day when I retire, I will…"

"One day when I marry the perfect husband, I will …"

The fact of the matter is that these things may never happen. 'One day' and 'someday' promises that you make to yourself are completely based on chance. So, who is your Gogo Maggie? What are you waiting for? Why pin your dream on things you have no control over? You must wake up and start living your life fully right now.

1. Gogo: In South Africa, Gogo is an endearing term for Grandmother.

"Someday is not a day of the week," said romance novelist Janet Dailey. She went from secretary to bestselling author with millions of copies of her books sold worldwide. During her most prolific years, Dailey set herself the goal of writing 15 pages per day. Her day began at 4 a.m. Some of her early novels took only eight days to write. She clearly didn't wait for 'someday', but rather stuck to a routine with self-discipline – and later reaped the rewards.

The reason why most people die without having used the talents and gifts that they were born with, is because they get stuck in a habit of putting things off until time runs out on them.

It is said that people who cry the loudest on their deathbeds are people that never truly lived. They are observers of life, but not participants. They take no risks; they merely stand on the sidelines watching. If you keep on putting things off, procrastinating, that's what will happen to you too! You will deprive everyone of your talents and gifts that can make this world a better place. So, wake up and do what you came here to do and make a difference in the world.

Dealing with procrastination requires a deep understanding of its underlying causes. Excuses like, "I am not in the mood to start" or "I will begin tomorrow" are not by any means the cause of procrastination. They are just deceits that we use to make ourselves feel less guilty.

So allow me to help you overcome some deceitful excuses right here and right now:

## 1. I can't do it because it will take a long time

If you really want to improve your life, it does not matter how long it will take. Often it takes something or someone outside of you to help you realise that. Dr Murray Banks a sought-after psychiatrist and motivational speaker who died in 2008, had the following exchange between himself and a woman who decided not to return to university because she would be too old when she finished.

"How old would you be in five years if you got that degree by starting now?, he asked her. "Forty-nine," she replied. "And how old will you be in five years if you don't go back to school?" "Forty-nine." she answerd, and became conscious of the excuses she had created for not elevating her life.

However long it took you to create any self-defeating habit, you did it all one day, one moment at a time. "A journey of a thousand miles begins with a single step," said Chinese philosopher Lao-tzu.

## 2. I can't do it because I can't afford it

Most people focus on the price of getting something and

they forget about how much it costs them to not have it. If one looks at the price of attaining a degree, it may seem pricey, but if you don't pay for it, it may cost you many rands in missed opportunities in the long run. So, don't be penny-wise and pound-foolish. There is no amount that is bigger than a dream that is unfulfilled.

### 3. I can't do it because no one is willing to help me

The world is filled with people who would jump at the chance to help you with whatever you'd like to create. But if you hold on to a false notion that no one will be there to help you, then your experiences will match that belief.

Sometimes you have to stand up to that voice in your head that keeps on talking you out of your dreams, saying you are not good enough, or you don't deserve your dream.

### 4. I can't do it because it has never been done before

Think of Roger Bannister who completed a mile in less than four minutes in 1954, something unheard of at the time. The Wright brothers in December 1903 flew their fly machine, the first in the world. People said it couldn't be done, never mind that it hadn't been done before. These people changed the world.

Just imagine the missed opportunities had these men entertained the idea that it had not been done before.

Jim Rohn said, "It's not what happens to us, it is what we choose to do about what happens that makes the difference in how our lives turn out."

I tell people that if something has never been done before, I have arrived to make it happen. This attitude has propelled me to do things that I hadn't dreamed of ever doing. I have experienced that when one commits oneself, providence moves too, and all sorts of things magically fall into place to help one achieve things. If something has never happened before, that is all the more reason for you to make it happen now. Please cease to be the slave of your past!

### 5. I can't do it because I am too old or too young

You have probably heard statements such as: "You can't fall in love again at your age" or "You can't change occupations because you are past your prime" or "It's too late to write the book you've always wanted to write", and of course, "You can't teach an old dog new tricks." This is an insult even to an old dog.

You can do whatever you want to do, as long as you have a will and determination to do it. There are so many stories about young people achieving remarkable things and old people doing things they shouldn't do at their age. Take for example the Brazilian granny Aida Mendes who decided to do skydiving in her later years. After her jump, she is quoted as having said: "In life you have to be brave, courage is always useful." She was 100 years old at the time.

What other mind viruses and excuses have you picked up that are putting brakes in your life? Most people go through life with their brakes on, making it difficult to move forward in life and reach their greatness.

The solution to procrastination is to identify and deal with your personal 'brakes' and mind viruses. They cause your inability to complete a task; it is not the difficulty of the task that holds you back.

Respected German psychotherapist Fritz Perls pointed out. "It's the awareness of how you are stuck, that makes you recover." It is lifelong, set-in-stone thinking that keeps you stuck ... often without you realising that you are stuck!

Since this type of mental activity can't lead you in a new direction, becoming aware must be the first step to getting rid of your excuses forever. Breaking old habits requires noticing that you're creating impediments in your life.

Awareness will remind you of what you are capable of becoming. Awareness allows you to perceive possibilities rather than see difficulties. Visualize yourself as the person you intend to be in future. Your self-image, the way you see yourself on the inside, largely determines your performance on the outside. Most Improvements in your outer life begin with improvements on the inside, in your mental picture.

Let us follow Jim Rohn's wise advice: "Let others lead small lives, but not you. Let others argue over small things, but not you. Let others cry over small hurts, but not you. Let others leave their future in someone else's hands, but not you."

# Healthy Is Indeed Wealthy

*"If you want to change the fruits, you will first have to change the roots. If you want to change the visible, you must first change the invisible."*

~T. Harv Erker

Healthy is wealthy - and wealthy is healthy. Have you ever allowed the full meaning of these words to sink in to the depths of your mind and soul?

Human beings are part of nature, not above it. Consequently, when we align with the laws of nature and work on our roots – our inner world – our life flows smoothly. When we don't, life gets rough.

Let's go scientific for a moment and look at plants: you plant a seed and provide sunlight, water and fresh air for the plant to grow. After that the embryo passes into the growth stage known as germination and enlarges, bursting out of the seed coating. The first growth is downward, creating the plant's main root.

Once the root establishes a hold in the soil, the plant grows upwards and eventually emerges above the ground. Small leaves start appearing quickly on the stems to make food for the plant. After considerable growth, the plant starts bearing fruit.

In every forest, on every farm and in every garden on earth, it is what's under the ground that creates what's above the ground. You cannot change the fruits that are already hanging on a tree. You can, however, change the fruits that are still to come. But to do so, you will have to strengthen and feed the roots (that is why we have fertiliser, compost etc).

The reason why I am telling you this, is that we have more in common with plants than we may realise. Many of us don't succeed because we deviate from natural laws, we focus on the fruits rather than on the roots.

Like plants need certain conditions to grow and bear good fruits, human beings need spiritual, mental, emotional and physical wellbeing if we are to succeed in life. Like plants, humans need pruning occasionally – that is, cutting out bad habits, unhealthy foods and limiting beliefs.

Like plants, we need to strengthen and feed our roots. Because we live in a world of cause and effect (duality), our 'fruit' or success depends heavily on our healthy roots and our overall wellbeing.

So, if you are not happy with your fruit or success, go fetch the fertiliser and the pruning shears and let's start making changes.

**Spiritual health** – it doesn't really matter what spiritual beliefs you hold and what church you belong to or not. We are spiritual beings and you need to feed your soul:

- Pray and meditate often.
- Socialise with people who share the same beliefs.
- If you are religious, study your holy books of preference like the Bible, the Qu'ran and others.
- Don't simply stand on the sidelines but practise what you believe in; attend gatherings, go on pilgrimages, and observe traditional festivals and days of observance.
- Live according to your own core beliefs, values and purpose.

**Mental health** – the human mind is important and powerful, what a pity we only use about 10 percent of it! This is where your beliefs, thoughts, and values reside. These lead to your action, behaviour, and ultimately your destiny.

This is your soil, whatever you plant in it grows - but remember that weeds grow without being planted and you have to keep on eradicating them. Mahatma Gandhi wrote: "Your beliefs become your thoughts, Your thoughts become your words, Your words become your actions, Your actions become your habits, Your habits become your values, Your values become your destiny."

Some ideas on how you can feed and improve your mental health:

- Expose your mind to positive messages early in the morning, as this will set the tone of your day. You can use positive affirmations like, "Good things are supposed to happen to me!"

This will create a sense of entitlement in your mind and will focus you on creating and attracting good things to your life.

- Read biographies about successful people and you will see that ordinary people like you can do extraordinary things. See that you don't need to be great to get started, but you have to get started to be great.
- Do mental detoxification. Albert Einstein was right when he said, "The thinking that got us here isn't the thinking that's going to get us where we need to be." It's important to note that some people's thinking and habits won't support you to your next goal, so get rid of them, do some pruning.
- Play games like puzzles, chess, Sudoku, and other brain teasers. This will improve your

IQ, memory and alertness, among others.
- Plan out your day, and set goals. But don't stress out if you don't accomplish everything the way you planned. Remain flexible and try different approaches to your goals. Remember, sometimes life happens, and you may not have time for everything. Just be productive in the time you have.
- Go out and do activities to find what you like and then pursue the one or two that strike your fancy. Don't do too many.
- Keep a diary or journal. This would be a good place to write things. But remember, no negative thoughts.
- Pick a hobby that you enjoy.
- Hobbies can counter daily stress.
- Laugh out loud as often as you can as it releases feel-good hormones.

**Physical health** – you have to feed your body with good and healthy food and drink enough water to cleanse the body of all the unwanted toxins. Much has been said and written about this topic, but allow me to remind you of some essential basics:

- Get sufficient exercise. Choose whatever suits your body, your lifestyle and your budget best. If you have a disability, you can adopt a modified exercise regimen.

- Get sufficient rest. About eight hours of sleep helps the body repair itself. You may personally need more or less, as sleep requirements vary between people.
- Eat healthier. Stick to a balanced diet that consists of fruit, vegetables, fish, chicken and red meat (or alternative protein if you're vegan/vegetarian). Look online and find the food pyramid, then try balancing your caloric intake with your exercise.
- Find time to relax. Just lie down and think about what you did before you started relaxing. Think positive thoughts or take up a relaxing hobby.
- Spend time in nature because you need sun and fresh air like plants do.
- Do some de-stressing breathing exercises.
- Laugh out loud as often as you can as it exercises your diaphragm and your stomach muscles.

**Emotional and social health** – our emotional wellbeing is tied to our spiritual, physical and mental health. Take good care of them so that you can remain emotionally healthy. The essential basics here include, among others:

- Having good relationships at work, at home and in society at large. "Deeply connecting with others and noting how you can be of service to them is today's currency for success," says Dr Jonathan D Moch in his

book Health is Wealth.
- Getting out of toxic relationships.
- Being socially active; join groups of people where you can have face-to-face interaction. With the advent of social media, we have become isolated and too lazy to go out and seek physical contact and conversation with others.
- Managing stress.
- Laughing out loud.
- Generally having fun.

Canadian pastoral worker A.J. Reb Materi summarised it best with: "So many people spend their health gaining wealth, and then have to spend their wealth to regain their health."

# Reinventing Yourself Step-By-Step

*"Imagination is more important than knowledge. Knowledge is limited. Imagination encircles the world"*

~ Albert Einstein

Everybody does it at some stage – upgrade. We do it with phones, we do it with cars and with houses. We upgrade our CVs and our clothes and our hairstyles. And guess what? We also have to upgrade our goals, our thinking and our lives.

Once you have achieved one set of goals, you have to move on. Reinventing yourself is all about upgrading; about becoming more and better than you were previously. It is about climbing to the next level.

Our beloved father of the nation, Nelson Mandela, explained that once you reach the top of a mountain, you realise that there are many other mountains to climb.

Why limit yourself to only one mountain? Ask yourself:

- Am I still on track regarding the purpose of my life?
- How can I be healthier?
- How can I improve my life?
- How can I be more knowledgeable?
- How can I be more productive?
- How can I be more resourceful?
- How can I grow?
- How can I contribute more to society?
- Whom can I help?
- Where else can I make a difference?

Asking yourself these critical questions will ensure that you keep searching for ways to improve yourself and your life. Yes, it is easier to stay stuck on the same level. Yes, it takes effort to re-invent yourself. But do it in anyway.

When I started my own company, I worked from home. I did that for almost a year. I then moved to an office that I shared with a friend, and that changed my thinking about the possibility of owning my own office one day. I kept wondering how and what I could upgrade in my life. I started with myself – I started reading more books on motivation, attended seminars and workshops and classes. I also joined Alberton Toastmasters Club.

Two years later, my questioning, "How can I be more

than I am right now?" prompted me to move on again.

I worked hard at becoming more resourceful, invested in becoming a better person and as a result started attracting more business. It is important to note that business opportunities do not just happen; we attract them.

When you work hard on yourself, you attract wonderful people, situations and opportunities you never anticipated! That is what has been happening to me. I remember vividly when my mindset changed: I attended a three-day National Achievers Congress (NAC) seminar in Sandton Convention Centre in July 2013. This seminar changed the way I thought about life, I met the likes of Robert Kiyosaki, Gerry Roberts, Courtney Smith, and Les Brown, the man that I had dreamt of meeting one day. Not only did I meet him, but he has since then become my personal mentor.

I am living my dream presently. Yet note that I relentlessly ask myself how I can be more. Somehow, recently, the opportunity to own my own office fell from the sky and I grabbed it. While raising the bar on myself, I decided to undertake an assignment I had thought was impossible for me – writing this book. Talk about stepping outside my comfort zone! Yet, here you are reading my book.

Your true happiness and potential is found outside your comfort zone says Brian Tracey. He calls it the "Danger

Zone" because you become so comfortable there that you get stuck.

Many of us don't go to the next level of our greatness because of self- doubt and we stay stuck. We are all born to be great and greatness is a choice we have to make every day.

By continuously challenging and raising the bar on yourself, you discover parts of you that you never knew ... Your true life happens outside the 'danger zone'.

Imagine yourself bigger and better and higher up on Mandela's proverbial mountain. As George Bernard Shaw said, "Life isn't about finding yourself. Life is about creating yourself."

# Reinventing yourself step-by-step exercise

1. Take stock of your life.

2. Identify the gap from where you are and where you want to be.

3. Write your findings/gap down.

4. Establish what needs to be done to close this gap.

5. Set a goal for each finding and go for it.

6. Acknowledge that you are what you are and where you are because of what went through your mind. Acknowledge that you can change your mindset and change your life.

7. Invest more in yourself by reading books, listening to CDs, attending seminars, workshops and classes. Surround yourself with people who will support you, inspire you and bring something to the table.

8. Make a list and then let go of people and things that hold you back. "Life is like an elevator: on your way up, sometimes, you have to stop and

let some people off." ~ Unknown.

9. Reach out and allow new people into your life.

10. Monitor the results and keep adjusting where necessary. The new you will emerge and the results will show.

"Do not go where the path may lead, go instead where there is no path and leave a trail." ~ Ralph Waldo Emerson

# Secret Success Formula

**"Be yourself; everyone else is already taken."** ~ Oscar Wilde

I spent a few years searching for success. I was hoping to find it in a tall, fancy bottle, beautifully labelled of course, and at a good price. But none of the shops stock it, as you yourself have probably noticed.

I then went on to discover the reason why shops don't sell bottled success. It is because every human being has what it takes to make his or her own success! Who needs a bottle of success when you have the formula to make your own magic muti?

My personal formula is called Veli. Graciously allow me to tell you about Veli

**'V'** is for visualise. You have to visualise what it is you want to achieve. Have you ever thought of somebody and the person phones you out of the blue or you bump into him or her? This proves that our thoughts have magnetic power, what we think about, we bring about. As you think about your goals and dreams, hold a vision of what you want to achieve. Do the goal setting exercise in Chapter 5 and once you have identified your goals, carry the list with you so that you can remind yourself of your major goal.

Do it as often as you'd like, but do it at least three times daily. We are busy being and we tend to forget things in the course of our busyness. 2. Muti is a South African common term for medicine.

When you wake up in the morning you can use the mantra "Good things are supposed to happen to me!"

This will further drive it to your subconscious mind where belief is created that you deserve success - and it will manifest itself. To further kick-start your day on the right track, write down ideas that will help you achieve your goal, don't try to quantify or qualify them. Let the ideas flow and incorporate them into your day if possible. Who knows, one of these ideas may change your life. 'V' is also for victory – the victory of achieving that which we visualise.

**'E'** is for expanding your goals. People fail in life not because they aim too high and miss. No, they fail in life because they aim too low and hit. Some don't even aim at all. So, you have to raise the bar on yourself. Why is that important? Because in order to do something you have never done before, you have to become someone you have never been. When you expand your goals, you start to introduce yourself to a part of yourself that you didn't know existed. Don't go to your grave leaving a life of mediocrity behind because you were too scared to step out of your comfort zone. Brian Tracey calls the comfort zone 'the danger zone' because people learn to become comfortable with their discomforts and end up settling for the crumbs of life.

We have to take risks. Les Brown says, "If you are not willing to risk, you cannot grow, if you cannot grow you cannot be your best, if you cannot be your best you cannot be happy and if you cannot be happy, then what else is there?"

And you have to love what Helen Keller said: "Life is too short and unpredictable, please eat the dessert first!" When you look at your goals and dreams, dare to expand on them. Dare to dream big. Dare to re-invent yourself. Stretch yourself and you'll discover abilities, talents and skills that have been lying dormant.


**'L'** is for leverage your relationships. You cannot make it by yourself. One goose can fly 75% further in a formation with other geese than it can fly by itself, did you know? Diana Nyad, an American record-setting long-distance swimmer was asked [after swimming 180 km from Cuba to Florida at the age of 64] how she did it and she said three things:

1. Never give up on your dreams
2. You are never too old to live your dream.
3. It may appear to be a solo act but it takes teamwork.

As you look at your goals and dreams, you will have to enrol people to support you. Leverage your relationships; pull OQP (Only Quality People).

Help those suffering from arrested development, but learn as much as you can from OQP. Learn all you can: Learners are high earners. Dennis Kimbro went as far as saying that if you are the smartest one in your group, you should get a new group. He is an educator and the author of What makes the great GREAT, a book that is well worth a read.

Look at your relationships and ask yourself what is this relationship doing to me? Am I growing spiritually, mentally, emotionally and financially? You want to be around people that you can learn from. Your network creates your net worth.

Know that if you are not growing you are dying. When you surround yourself with people you can learn from, you can change the course of your history. Show me the books you read and your five closest friends and I can predict your income and your future.

There are many people who cannot achieve their goals

because they have too many toxic, negative, energy-draining people in their lives.

Create collaborative achievement-driven relationships. Surround yourself with people that will complement you, people that will bring something to the table the same as you.

In his book called Average is Over, Thomas Friedman writes, "In the past, workers with average skills, doing an average job, could earn an average lifestyle. But, today, average is officially over. Being average just won't earn you what it used to. It can't when so many more employers have so much more access to so much more above average cheap foreign labour, cheap robotics, cheap software, cheap automation and cheap genius. Therefore, everyone needs to find their extra — their unique value contribution that makes them stand out in whatever is their field of employment."

Average is over. The people that are going to make it and control their financial future are the people who develop their skills set and develop themselves so they complement technology.

Experts claim that in the next decade, 85 percent of people will be threatened by technology and outsourcing because they have not invested in further learning. You have got to continue upgrading your knowledge.

Retired (deep in his 80s) American televangelist and motivational speaker, Robert Schuller was right when he said you either expand or you are expendable (replaceable). As we look at ourselves and look at our great country South Africa, we need to continue learning so that we can become competitive global citizens.

**'I'** is for imagination. He may have been one of the greatest scientists humanity has ever produced, but Albert Einstein loved imagination more than he loved facts. He said that imagination is more powerful than knowledge and that it is the preview of what's to come.

You cannot succeed when you are living out of your history rather than out of your imagination. You have to look at where you are going; you got to begin to anticipate what's coming. How can you position yourself so you can take advantage of what's there?

At the age of 24, John H. Johnson founder of Johnson Publishing Co, tried to find a bank that would loan him some money. He was waved away by bankers who contemptuously called him 'boy'.

Undaunted, Johnson decided to go directly to the public for start-up money. Putting down his mother's furniture as collateral, he borrowed

$500. Because of his imagination, he believed in the future. He now owns a $400-million empire publishing

Ebony and Jet magazines. Entrepreneurs are people that use their imagination; they don't look at things as they are but rather as they can be.

You cannot buy success ready-bottled off the shelf, but you can start today to:

**V**isualise what it is that you want...

**E**xpand your vision of yourself...

**L**everage your relationships... and use your

**I**magination to create your own success.

I hope that my humble success 'formula' will inspire you to dream big.

# Inspirational Stories – South African Rising Stars

There are many inspirational stories of young South Africans who are succeeding in a big way, but I would like to mention three here. Read more about these under-30 South Africans and be inspired.

I don't know him personally, but I have seen him on television Jerome 'Slim' du Plooy. He chose the nicname Slim because he has a slim, slight body and because it stands for what he believes in, namely Success Lies In Me.

Slim grew up in Kliptown, Soweto, with his single mom. They lived without electricity for 16 years and faced many trials and tribulations. However, Slim remained dedicated to his schooling and completed high school with good marks. While still at school, he attended the Soweto Kliptown Youth (SKY) afterschool program sponsored by the NBA (American National Basketball Association) and took up basketball. Slim loved playing basketball and talking about basketball - this was the beginning of a great passion.

Great things followed: the NBA took him on a trip to America and sponsored his academic studies at Boston Media House in Johannesburg. In 2009, he graduated with a Boston diploma in media, majoring in radio broadcasting. Today, Slim du Plooy is a sought-after MC, actor, radio and television personality as well as a motivational speaker and a brand ambassador for Nike SA.

He has represented SA on the NBA global basketball development programme called Basketball Without Borders, where he rubbed shoulders with big names in basketball, such as Dwight Howard, Kyrie Irving and Caron Butler.

"I keep telling young people what I often tell myself: don't limit yourself, think big," says the 27 year-old Slim. "If you don't believe in yourself, how can you expect other people to believe in you? I keep dreaming big even when I'm down or struggling." Despite a busy schedule, Slim makes time to mentor and help youth from underprivileged backgrounds.

Pearl Thusi is another inspirational young South African. You can see Pearl on television and her face graces many top magazines. Pearl grew up in the rolling green hills of rural KwaZulu-Natal. She was a bit of a tomboy; chasing after chickens and an array of other domestic animals. Her mother passed away when Pearl was 16-years old. Pearl's father, a taxi owner and part-time bodybuilder, raised her and her six siblings.

Being more light-skinned compared to her brothers and sisters, as well as the other children in the township, Pearl was bullied and teased about her looks. The kids called her 'white cockroach'.

But Pearl didn't let the name or the teasing deter her

from becoming one of South Africa's sought-after black models and a respected TV presenter and actress. A failed relationship and getting pregnant at 18 were merely detours in the journey towards her dream. The going was tough, but Pearl kept persevering and never lost faith. She is 26 years old.

At only 25, Siyabulela Xuza is a science prodigy that many compare with Mark Shuttleworth. Born and bred in Mthatha, a small town in the Eastern Cape, Siya started experimenting with rocket fuel at the age of six. Why? He dreamed of going to Jupiter (seeing that the moon and Mars had already been reached by humans). He nearly blew up his mother's humble kitchen. After many failed attempts, he managed to produce rocket fuel by the age of 17 and went on to take the world by storm. His homemade rocket fuel won him the top prize in its category at the Intel International Science and Engineering Fair in the United States. He was also awarded a scholarship to study engineering at Harvard University.

In 2011 he became a fellow of the Kairos Society, a global network of top student and global leaders using entrepreneurship and innovation to solve the world's greatest challenges.

He was invited to the United Nations and the New York Stock Exchange in recognition for being one of the world's emerging business leaders and to offer strategies for solving the world's energy crisis.

Siya is presently working on his own start-up, an energy solution company and gives innovation-themed talks around South Africa, where he is now permanently based. Though he never got to Jupiter, he tells audiences, he has had a minor planet named after him as recognition for his scientific work. He is the ultimate believer in dreaming big and aiming high.

# Taking Responsibility for You

"People are always blaming their circumstances for what they are. I don't believe in circumstances. The people who get on in this world are the people who get up and look for the circumstances they want, and, if they can't find them, they make them." ~ George Bernard Shaw

You and only you are responsible for your life. Period. It's not your parents, your past relationships, your job, the economy, the government, employer, company policy, weather, bank (for not lending you the money you need), or your age that is to blame.

It is a waste of time pointing fingers and blaming things and people for your failures and shortcomings. We like finger pointing because it is easier to find someone to blame than it is to fix the problem, isn't it?

It is true that we sometimes have to overcome huge challenges. It is true that we sometimes encounter people that hold us back. It is undeniably true that circumstances and random events sometimes hit us hard. That is how life is. However, you are still the boss of your life.

You have full responsibility over your dreams, you have to protect and nurture them, and don't let others kill or steal your dreams.

Monty Roberts reckons that some people are dream stealers. I listened to him give a talk on this topic. "When I was a high school student, there was a kid in my class who was itinerant; his dad was a trainer of horses and he never lived anywhere for longer than a couple of months," Monty told the audience. "He would stay at a school for a couple of months and then move on to the next school. He had a dream though; he wanted to raise racing horses. One day, a teacher asked the kids to write down what they wanted to be when they grew up, and he got very excited. He wrote that he wanted to raise racing horses, made sketches of a 200 hectare ranch and drew a diagram of 4000 square foot house and drew where the race track would be, the tack room, bunk house, central administration office, the whole lot. He handed it in and got it back a week later written "F, SEE ME AFTER CLASS".

He was shocked; he had poured his heart into this. He went to his teacher and asked why he got an F. The teacher said, "You are a poor kid living at the back of a truck, do you know what land costs in this valley, do you know what it costs for breeding stock and stock fees?

Your dream is an unrealistic dream for a young man like you. There is no way you can achieve this. It's my job as a teacher to make sure that you don't grow up and be disappointed. So, I want you to write a more realistic dream for yourself and I'll give you a higher grade.'" The student went home and thought about it. After a week, he went back to his teacher and handed back the same paper and said, "You can keep your F and I'll keep my dream."

The student was none other than Monty Roberts! Today he owns a ranch that looks exactly as he had presented it to his teacher and makes millions of dollars in profit. Known as the 'Man Who Listens to Horses', he is an award-winning trainer of championship horses, best-selling author, Hollywood stunt man, foster dad to 47 children (in addition to three of his own) and creator of the world-renowned and revolutionary equine training technique called Join~Up.

It is critical to ask yourself every day how much progress you are making. We have limited time on this planet, so waiting for something to happen won't help you; more so seeing that none of us know when we are going to depart.

It is said that people give reasons because they don't have the results and those who have the results don't need to give reasons.

My advice for you is to stop blaming, complaining, or criticising! These activities drain your energy and make you sick. Accept full responsibility for everything in your life, whether you caused it or not; even external problems can have internal solutions. Taking responsibility for your life will empower you, foster success, and heighten self-esteem, all of which lead to increased happiness.

Think of yourself as a creator, not a victim. Accept responsibility for who you are, who you will become, the choices you make, and the consequences that result. Hold yourself accountable. My mentor, Les Brown says, "Accept responsibility for your own life. Know that it is you who will get you where you want to go, no one else."

Listen to the little voice in your head. And, observe yourself talking with co-workers, family members, and friends. Do you hear yourself taking responsibility or placing blame? Let me repeat it: no one can live your life for you. You are in charge. Remember that today's decisions are tomorrow's realities.

No matter how hard you try to blame others for the events of your life, each event is the result of choices you made or failed to make. When you don't make a choice, other people choose on your behalf. And that can be a disaster because they don't necessarily have your interest at heart and they don't care about your dreams either.

Look at it this way: when you eat out, you have to choose which restaurant you want to go to. When you get there you choose where you want to sit and who you want to sit with, and you get a menu to choose what you want to eat and what you choose is entirely up to you. If you give your power away and allow someone else to choose on your behalf, you may not like what lands in your plate.

A restaurant represents life and a menu represents the choices you face on a daily basis. You can choose what to read, what thoughts to create, whom to befriend, where to go, what to listen to, and how much success you want to have.

To help you develop an attitude and habit of taking responsibility, try the following:

- First, listen to the voice in your head. Eliminate blame; eliminate excuses. If the blame track or the excuse track plays repeatedly in your mind, you are shifting responsibility for your decisions and life to others.
- Second, listen to yourself when you speak. In your conversation, do you hear yourself blame others for things that don't go exactly as you want? Do you find yourself pointing fingers at your co-workers or your

upbringing, your parent's influence, the amount of money that you make, or your spouse?

- Are you making excuses for goals unmet or tasks that missed their deadlines? If you can hear your blaming patterns, you can stop them.
- Third, if an individual you respect supplies feedback that you make excuses and blame others for your woes, take the feedback seriously. Control your defensive reaction and explore examples and deepen your understanding with the co-worker or friend.

Sidney Poitier wrote in his book The Measure of a Man that something happens when you walk with someone. Either you adjust your pace to theirs, or they adjust to yours.

Whose responsibility is it to set the pace? Whose pace have you adjusted to? It is best you walk with winners.

# A note on winning

***"Winning lifts everyone it touches – it just makes the world a better place."*** ~ Jack Welch

I hope you enjoy reading this book as much as I enjoyed writing it. I urge you to think and live like a winner. I urge you to want more in life. There's nothing wrong with wanting more in life, as long as you're enjoying the things God has already given you, and you're sharing them with others.

Winners work hard and I encourage you to work hard. "Whatever you do, work with all your heart, as working for the Lord, not for men," says Apostle Paul in Colossians 3:23, in the Holy Bible.

I don't know your definition of winning. But in my book, winning does not refer to winning a race. It does not refer to cold ambition to become better than other people. It is not about ego or boasting. Winning is also not synonymous with competition. Winning is more than that.

Timothy Webster summarises it succinctly in his book, Thinking about YOU: "It is possible to come in first place and still lose. If you partake in a race where the competition is inferior, it will be relatively easy to outshine the rest … Winning means stretching your boundaries, striving for excellence and always being prepared. More importantly, winning has an unselfish trait that allows you to provide for other people."

# Acknowledgements

Without the following people, this book would not have been possible:

My family - My late dear Mom Ellen Ntombini Ndaba and my Great Aunt Catherine Thembani Nkosi, these two women shaped my life and made me the man I am and I will forever be indebted to their teachings about humility and love. My wife Mpumi Ndaba and our two lovely boys Ntokozo and Sanele Ndaba who believe in me and stand by me no matter what. My late brother Sydney Ndaba, my sister Deborah Ndaba, and my brother Joshua Ndaba.

Friends and associates -James Mpele, Bangani Ngeleza, Themba Nkosi (of Impumelelo), and Carina van der Walt.

The professional team behind this book - Eulália Snyman, Dylan Fourie, Maria Capazario and Marco van der Walt.

My mentors - Les Brown, Sofia Tasker and Ronnie Martin. All the people that have made a contribution and have helped to shape the person I have become, thank you, thank you! Thank you Lord Yaweh. I love you all. I thank everyone from the bottom of my heart.

To you reading this book – blessings.

Veli Ndaba 2014

# References and suggested reading

**Help! I'm Going CRAZY!** – by Terri Ann Laws

**As a Man Thinketh** – by James Allen

**The Richest Man in Babylon** – by George S Clason

**The Greatest Salesman in the World** – by Og Mandino

**Think and Grow Rich** – by Napoleon Hill **Excuses Begone!** – by Dr Wayne W Dyer **Walking with Tigers** – by Frank Furness
**Secrets of the Millionaire Mind** – by T. Harv Erker

**The Leader Who Had No Title** – by Robin Sharma

**Tough times never last, but tough people do!** – by Robert H Schuller

**Thinking about YOU** – by Timothy Webster

**Man's Search for Meaning** – by Viktor Frankl The Holy Bible
**Awaken the Giant Within** – by Tony Robbins **The Measure of a Man** – by Sidney Poitier **Own your Industry** – by Douglas Kruger **Long Walk to Freedom** – by Nelson Mandela

**Five major Pieces to the Life Puzzle** – by Jim Rohn

**The University of Success** – by Og Mandino

**What makes the great GREAT** – by Dennis Kimbro

**David & Goliath, underdogs, misfits and the art of battling giants**
– by Malcolm Gladwell

**Winning** – by Jack Welch

**Who moved my cheese?** – by Dr Spencer Johnson

**Personal Greatness** – by Rinus le Roux

**7 Habits of Highly Effective People** – Stephen Covey

**Health is Wealth, Confronting Uncomfortable Truths** – by Jonathan D Moch
**It's Not Over Until You Win: How to Become the Person You Always Wanted to Be No Matter What the Obstacle** – by Les Brown
**Live your dreams** – by Les Brown

**Advice on Dying and Living a Better Life** – by the Dalai Lama

**No Man is an Island** – by Thomas Merton The Power of Now – by Eckhart Tolle Acres of Diamonds – by Russell Conwell

www.ingramcontent.com/pod-product-compliance
Lightning Source LLC
Chambersburg PA
CBHW032133090426
42743CB00007B/583